Journey To The Black Hole

Kabir Singh Rai

INDIA · SINGAPORE · MALAYSIA

ISBN 979-8-89673-736-0

This book belongs to:

"Look at the sky. We are not alone. The whole universe is friendly to us and conspires only to give the best to those who dream and work." - Dr. A.P.J Abdul Kalam

Thoughts by Me-Kabir Singh Rai

Designed by my Mom

Executed by my Papa

I am so
GRATEFUL

Acknowledgment

This book is special to me because of so
many wonderful people!

Thank you to my grandparents for always
believing in me and teaching me cool things.
Big hugs to my mom and papa for loving me
and making me who I am.

I'm grateful to my school's Director
Rupa Chakravarty Ma'am,
Vice-Principal EYP Sangeeta Bagchi Ma'am,
and all my teachers for making learning fun.

A special thanks to Ruchi Mehra Ma'am for her
persistent encouragement.
To my friends and family, thank you for
being part of my Journey.

This book is here because of all of you.
Thank you to the universe
and beyond!

About the Author

Meet Kabir, a remarkable six-year-old whose fascination with the universe began when he was just three years old. While the world was hunkered down at home, grappling with the fear of the coronavirus, Kabir's curiosity about the cosmos only grew. His insightful questions about the stars, planets, and the mysteries of space led him on a journey to learn about the Big Bang, the solar system, and so much more. Long before his grandparents could sing him the lullaby "Chanda Mama," Kabir already knew that the moon is Earth's natural satellite. His parents and teachers quickly recognized his exceptional talent and boundless curiosity, encouraging him to write a book about one of his favorite topics—black holes. With a mind as vast as the universe itself, Kabir's book is a testament to his passion for learning and his incredible ability to grasp complex concepts at such a young age.

Contents

It's me, a black hole.

Today we are going to learn about black holes, one of the most mysterious objects that exist in the Universe.

A black hole is a place in space where gravity is so strong that even light cannot escape it.

But do you know

how do black holes form?

Black holes can form at the end of a star's life.

When a big star runs out of fuel, it no longer has the energy to hold the gravitational forces running inside it.

the core of a star collapses under its own weight, which is eight times more than the Sun's mass.

And It all happens in mili-seconds.

It causes a massive explosion which is billions of times brighter than the Sun.

This huge explosion is called a **Supernova**.

the remaining material from the explosion collapses into an infinitely dense point at the center of the black hole, known as the Singularity.

And this gives birth to a black hole.

There are four main types of black holes:

The first are the **Primordial black holes.**

These tiny black holes are thought to have formed very early in the universe, Just a fraction of a second after the **Big Bang**.

The second type of black holes are the Intermediate-mass.

These black holes range from about a mass between 100 and 100,000 times that of the Sun.

This mass range is higher than stellar black holes, but lower than supermassive black holes.

The third are the Stellar-mass black holes.

They are small in size and stretch around 20-100 miles across.

Stellar black holes typically weigh between 5 and 50 times the mass of the Sun.

Gaia-BH3, is the largest stellar black hole in the Milky Way galaxy and the second-closest black hole to Earth.

Gaia-BH3 is 33 times the mass of the Sun. It is 3000 light years from earth.

And the fourth type of black holes are the **Supermassive black holes**.

they are the largest types of black holes with masses ranging from millions to billions of times the mass of the Sun.

Supermassive black holes are mostly found in the center of large galaxies, where they hold the galaxy together.

Sagittarius A is the supermassive black hole at the center of our Milky Way galaxy, which is about 26,000 light-years from Earth.

What if you fell into a black hole?

The boundary of a black hole is known as the Event Horizon.

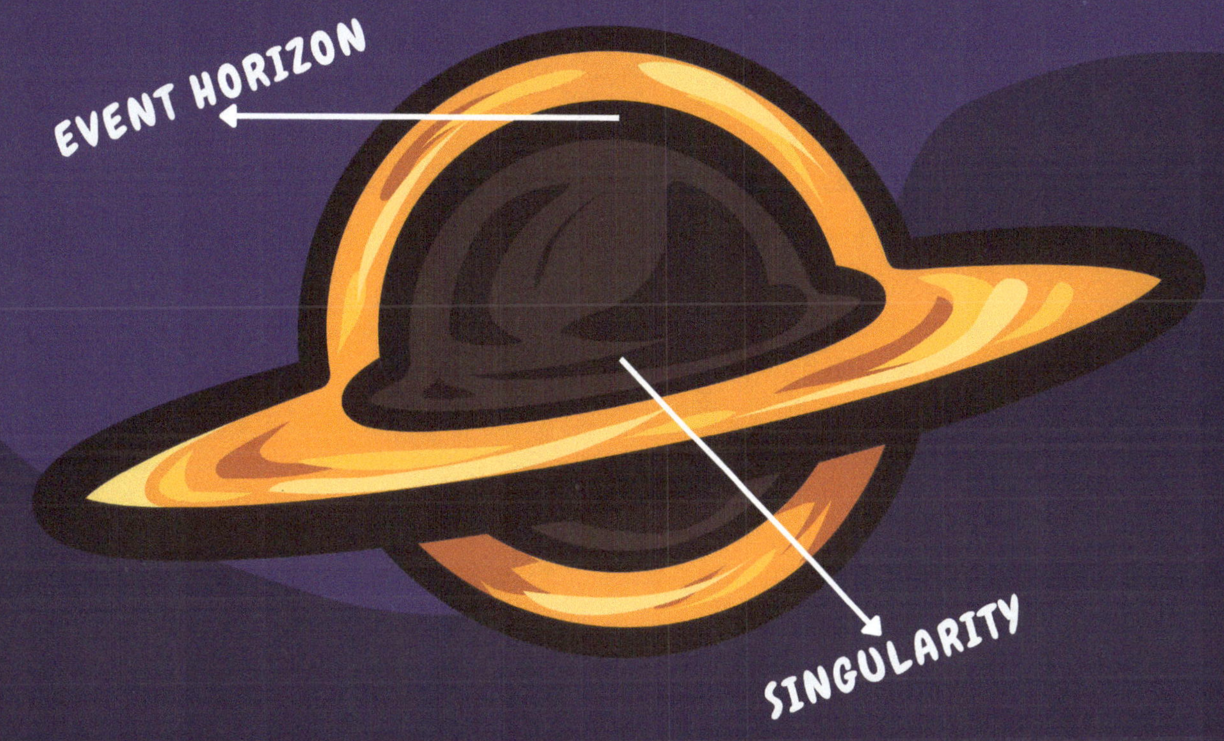

The gravity is so strong here that if anything tries to cross over, it will get sucked into a black hole. Even light cannot escape it.

Small black holes have stronger gravitational forces.

If you fell into a small black hole, strong gravitational forces will stretch you like a spaghetti noodle until you are torn apart, even before you cross the event horizon.

This process is called **spaghettification**.

Large black holes have less gravitational forces.

If you fell into a supermassive black hole, it is possible to pass the event horizon unharmed.

You would fall freely and reach to the point of singularity. Here you will get squeezed and merged into it.

Wow, that was such an interesting information. I am certainly curious to know more.

What will happen if two black holes collide ?

Black holes and black hole mergers are so dark, that you cannot even see them with telescopes.

When two black holes collide, they merge into one larger black hole.

It would produce a tremendous amount of energy and send massive ripples in space.

These ripples are called gravitational waves.

Are black holes dangerous for Planet Earth?

The closest stellar mass black hole to Earth is Gaia-BH1.

It is 1,560 light-years away from Planet earth, which is about 30 million years of travel time by rocket.

It is safe to say that black holes do not pose any threat to Earth.

What if the Sun turned into a black hole?

Don't worry! The Sun isn't big enough to turn into a black hole. Instead, it will become a red giant and later a white dwarf, which isn't dangerous at all.

But let's imagine what would happen if the Sun turned into a black hole.

The Sun wouldn't suddenly suck everything up like in the movies. Instead, it would shrink down into a very tiny, invisible point, but it would still have the same weight. The Earth and the other planets would still keep spinning around it, just like they do now. The big difference would be that without the Sun's light, it would get super dark and cold here on Earth.

The largest black hole ever discovered in the universe till now is Phoenix A. It has a mass of 100 billion Suns and it is almost 9 billion light years from Earth.

The second largest supermassive black hole in the universe is Ton-618. 66 billion Suns and almost 11 solar systems can fit into it.

Did you know?

There are billions of black holes in the universe, including Stellar-mass black holes, Supermassive black holes and Intermediate black holes.

If you fell into a black hole, you would never escape.

If you fell into a stellar-size black hole, you could turn into human spaghetti.

My dear friends, now it's time to return home, to Planet Earth.
What an incredible and adventurous journey it was!

GLOSSARY

Universe: Universe is a giant magical space which has everything. It has stars, planets, galaxies, energy, time and so many mysterious objects.

Supernova: When a big star runs out of fuel, it no longer has the energy to hold the gravitational forces running inside it. It causes a huge bright explosion and this explosion is called Supernova.

Big Bang: About 13.8 billion years ago the entire universe was squished inside a tiny hot bubble and then it suddenly exploded. This explosion made universe grow really big and created all the stars, planets and space we see today.

Singularity: An infinite dense point at the center of the black hole is called Singularity.

Galaxy: A galaxy is a huge group of stars, planets, gases and dust all held together by gravity in space. We live in the Milky Way galaxy.

Supermassive Black holes: They are the largest type of black holes and they can stretch up to billions of miles.

Event horizon: The boundary of a black hole is called event horizon. Gravity is so strong here that even light cannot escape it.

GLOSSARY

Spaghettification: Spaghettification is getting stretched out really really long because the black hole's gravity is so powerful and strong.

Gravity: Gravity is a force that pulls things towards each other.

Light year: Light year is a way to measure how far light can travel in one year.
One light year = 9 trillion kms.

White dwarf: When a star like the Sun gets really old, it runs out of fuel and can't keep shining the same way. So, it becomes a red giant and then shrinks down into a small, very hot, and super dense ball. This ball is called a white dwarf!

Let's colour it!

Let's colour it!

NOTES

NOTES

TO-DO

TO-DO

www.ingramcontent.com/pod-product-compliance
Lightning Source LLC
LaVergne TN
LVHW071124160826
845679LV00005B/1174

* 9 7 9 8 8 9 6 7 3 7 3 6 0 *